Gemstone & Crysta

Astrology

The

Secret code

"discover your true birthstone
your lucky Talisman"

Robert W Wood D.Hp
(Diploma in Hypnotherapy)

Rosewood Publishing

First published in U.K. 2002
By Rosewood Publishing
P.O. Box 219, Huddersfield,
West Yorkshire HD2 2YT

www.rosewood-gifts.co.uk

Robert W Wood D.Hp
Asserts the moral right to be identified
As the author of this work

Copy-editing
Margaret Wakefield BA (Hons) London
www.euroreportage.co.uk

Cover photograph by
Andrew Caveney BA (Hons)
www.andrewcaveneyphotography.co.uk

Cover and layout re-designed by
AJ Typesetting
www.ajtype.co.uk

Printed in Great Britain by
Delta Design & Print Ltd
www.deltaleeds.co.uk

ISBN 978-0-9532930-7-0   BK8

It was the Greeks that gave us the now-familiar twelve signs of the Zodiac, but it was Carl Gustav Jung who, at the turn of the twentieth century, successfully linked his special form of Psychology with Astrology.

The 'Mean Average'.

Many years ago I became involved in a project to try to find a list of twelve genuine Birthstones. It was for a new business venture, selling birthstone gifts through party plan. However, when I started to research into many different sources, I quickly realised that they all seemed to be saying something different. No two seemed to say the same thing. I studied and researched over 17 different sources for information, including encyclopaedias, world famous psychics, mystics and astrologers.

I discovered that different continents favoured their own 'home-grown' gemstones and crystals, and that it was only a few hundred years ago that people first discovered how to cut a diamond (it takes a diamond to cut a diamond). Astrology is over six thousand years old, which means that a diamond couldn't have been an original birthstone. In the end, because of all these different lists, I decided the only way would be to take the mean average. That is: if the majority of my differing sources said Red Jasper was the birthstone for Aries then that was good enough for me; and so this was how I got my list - by using the mean average.

Discovering the 'true' Birthstones.

Imagine: I now had a list of twelve stones - but was it the right list? How could I find out? I asked well over two thousand people to help with my research, to see if I had got it right (if anyone can get it right!). To test my list I decided to put all the birthstones, in the form of tumblestones, into a basket. Then I passed the basket around, at the same time asking everyone if they would select a stone that they liked. I also asked them to tell me their star signs. Surprisingly, as it turned out, sometimes as many as 70% seemed to pick out their own stones, but a bigger surprise was that of those who didn't pick out their own birthstone, many picked out their 'opposite'. That means, for example, if they were Aries, then instead of picking out Red Jasper (their own birthstone) they picked out Green Aventurine, their 'opposite' stone (Libra). *More later.*

A secret code.

During my research I came across the 'Law of Polarity'. This states that everything has an opposite - for example: night and day, hot and cold, right and wrong, Ying and Yang etc. In astrology it means the opposite star sign becomes very important. That is, *the meaning of one is enhanced by the knowledge of the other.* If you do read your horoscopes, why not in future, for fun, read both your own and your opposite star sign. It may help you to gain a fuller picture. A list of 'opposites' starts on page 12.

I wondered - could there be another explanation why so many people, during my tests, seemed to be connected one way or another to their own or opposite birthstones? The answer, I think, may be: by colour. For example, on my list Aries' birthstone is Red Jasper. Surprisingly, over the years, I have often heard people say they don't like the colour of their own birthstone; and whenever I hear this I always suggest to them that they are more likely, if they are Aries, to like green - knowing that Green Aventurine (Libra) is their opposite star sign.

Gemstones and the Bible.

During my research, a friend told me that I could find the gemstones and crystals that I was researching in the Bible - but no-one at the time seemed to know exactly where. Then a very strange thing happened. It was a Thursday morning, I remember; I acquired a Bible, and looking at the last page I realised there were nearly 1,400 pages. I was just thinking how overwhelming all this would be - where do you start to look for Gemstone-Crystals? - when this strange 'something' happened.

I was thumbing my way through the Bible when a page seemed to open up. I was drawn to a story in Exodus. It's all about God asking Aaron, who will become the first High Priest, to fashion a 'Breastpiece'. And on this 'Breastpiece' God instructed him to place twelve stones, saying that these twelve stones would represent the twelve tribes of Israel.

I thought, 'This is symbolism.' In astrology, twelve stones represent the cycle of life and are called birthstones. However, within hours on the same day, I was drawn to another page. This was in the New Testament (Rev. 21-19) where it talks about a New Jerusalem; and there's another list of twelve stones. Now this list is different from the first, but this second list is very interesting because Red Jasper, which by using the mean average I had chosen to represent Aries in Astrology, was the first foundation for the New Jerusalem in the Scriptures.

So, being curious, I read on, only to find that the sixth foundation for the New Jerusalem was Carnelian - and Carnelian was the birthstone I had picked for Virgo, the sixth sign in Astrology. The twelfth foundation was Amethyst - and Amethyst was the same gemstone I had picked for Pisces, the twelfth sign.

The right Birthstones.

Is there a 'right' list of twelve stones? That's what I was trying to find. My list of twelve had come about after a great deal of extensive research, and included a lot of practical experience in front of thousands of people from all kinds of backgrounds, all walks of life. Well over 100,000 people have now heard my talk on the mysteries that surround gemstones and crystals, a talk entitled 'Discover the hidden powers of Gemstones'. I have read books containing named lists of precious stones, semi-precious stones, some have even suggested rough stones, and even stones that can represent the first half of a star sign with a totally different one representing the second half of the sign. Confusing, isn't it!

It's strange to think now, but by taking the mean average I have probably come closer than many in finding the right twelve, if it's possible to find the right twelve; unfortunately even the Scriptures don't help to resolve this dilemma by having two different lists.

A lucky Birthstone-Talisman.

During my product research I designed what's now turned out to be one of my most popular gifts. It's a special pair of eardrops: a classic line with the star sign gemstone at the base and the opposite star sign stone above, with a spacer in between, on a sterling silver ear-wire. A talisman - a talisman is believed to protect the wearer from harm, and is thought to have magical powers. There's no stronger symbolism of the power of life than a birthstone, as it is a representation of our birth. Imagine all the power and energy that went into our  arrival here on earth. So birthstones seem to act as lucky talismans. The secret here is that we may have more than one birthstone: our own, plus our opposite.

The 'law of polarity': the meaning of one is enhanced by the knowledge of the other. So don't forget in future, if you do read your horoscope, to read your opposite star sign. It will help you to gain a fuller picture.

Where did all this start?

According to the best scholars, Planet Earth started around 4,500 million years ago. Plants and insects such as beetles have been around for over 450 million years. Dinosaurs became extinct 65 million years ago. And, if you believe in evolution, man may have been around for 1 or even 2 million years. However, I find this curious: although some fossil evidence seems to exist, there seems to be no record of man's existence until about 28,000 years BC. Cave drawings have been found that have been dated to about this time. It's almost as if a few thousand years ago, man, as we know him today, just turned up - from where, we don't know.

Here's a thought: a scientist spent many months below ground, enjoying all his home comforts - except that he didn't know the time. Left to his own devices, he reverted to a 25-hour, not a 24-hour, day.

In prehistoric times, people were nomadic, always moving from one camp to another, until about 6,000 years ago when they began to settle down and build. They started to farm the land, keep animals and grow crops. The first civilisation, as we would know it, was probably at Sumer, which was situated in a broad, fertile valley between the rivers Tigris and Euphrates. This area was known then as Mesopotamia and is now known as Iraq.

The beginning of Astrology.

It is around this time that men started to record, through writings, their thoughts about minerals, precious stones, aromatherapy and star gazing; all, probably, with a view to improving their lives, their crops and their health, whilst at the same time seeking to protect themselves from their enemies, whether human, natural or even supernatural. They were seeking to see into the future, and generally trying to discover the many secrets of the world and universe.

The High Priests, the holy and learned men of their time, were carefully observing the night skies and plotting the course of the stars. They were also the ones performing religious rites, worshipping all the many pagan gods by asking for help. They performed all kinds of ceremonies and rituals. From this kind of science came Astrology. No-one knows where this information came from, only that it came.

These sages and High Priests seemed to know a lot about the 'Dog Star' Sirius, known as Sirius A, and its smaller companion star Sirius B - despite the fact that these two bodies are right outside our own solar system. Sirius, the Dog Star, is the brightest star in the sky. The sages and High Priests thought that messengers from these systems had descended from the skies to earth to teach their ancestors good government and introduce them to a system for counting. This was at the time an intelligent interpretation of the facts then known.

Predicting the future.

Use your imagination - go back in time and imagine you have just arrived on the planet; it doesn't matter how, just that you have. You have no knowledge of Earth other than what you can see, touch, feel, taste and smell, but you do have one thing: your intelligence. You quickly realise that night follows day. After only a few years you will have noticed various seasons, each following on from the other; and so now you can see a pattern.

A logical start to this amazing 'pattern of life' would probably be soon after winter, around March or April, because then everything starts to grow. It then matures during summer, and bears fruit during autumn, before dying back in winter. Then this miracle of life starts all over again the following spring. So life is a cycle that repeats itself time after time after time. The Egyptian Priests took this knowledge and used it so accurately that they could foretell, each year, the flooding of the Nile to within a few days. Could this be the start of trying to see into the future?

The Birth of the Zodiac.

From 6,000 to 4,000 BC the Babylonians, Egyptians and Chinese all seem to have believed that the stars, representing the heavenly bodies, influenced the lives of all men.

The Babylonians, in particular, thought that the positions of the stars represented messages from the gods, and their Priests spent much of their lives studying with great care. They divided the heavens into regions, and various groups of stars into constellations, naming each one after their many different pagan gods or objects.

**Anybody who still thinks the sky is the limit
is short of imagination**

Around 600 BC, the Greeks re-named these constellations and gave them the now-familiar Twelve Signs of the Zodiac.

As the earth rotated through the year's cycle, the positions of each constellation seemed to indicate when men should plant seeds or reap harvests, when to stock fuels for winter, and so from these simple observations the science of Astrology was born. The Greeks believed that humans, as well as gemstones and crystals, were all born under the influence of the planets. So a person born under the sign of Pisces, for example, would share their sign with the gemstone Amethyst. Therefore Amethyst is thought to be particularly beneficial and can act as a lucky talisman for those born under the star sign of Pisces. *More about birthstones later.*

Modern Astrology.
From the beginning of our history right up to the seventeenth century, an astrological view of things was the accepted norm. This influence can still be seen today in the architecture of many of our great churches and cathedrals. The Zodiac window at Chartres in France is a fine example of what is commonly known as a 'rose window', normally based on the number twelve or even sometimes twenty-four. It should not be forgotten that the founders of modern Astronomy, such as Johannes Kepler, Galileo Galilei and many others, were all court astrologers in their time.

Carl Gustav Jung (1875-1961).
Much of the work of Carl Gustav Jung, a Swiss psychotherapist, was concerned with the symbolism of dreams, myths and religions. Up until the publication of his work on the Psychology of the Unconscious in 1911, Carl Gustav Jung had been a leading collaborator with Sigmund Freud. Freud is the founder of modern-day psychology, and along with Carl Jung was mainly responsible for the 20th century's fascination with the subconscious. For reasons still unknown, the time of birth and the placements of the planets can tell a skilled astrologer a great deal about an individual's temperament, talents and even their hang-ups.

You can benefit hugely from this knowledge. Even the Church uses it. Astonishingly, they have discovered that it's possible to separate the physical from the spiritual. The Church knows this through the workings of 'Myers Briggs typology', developed by a mother-and-daughter team from America, who took the work of Carl Young and expanded on it. If you ever get the chance to go on a Myers-Briggs course, I can highly recommend it.

Psychological profiling and Astrology

Carl Jung's research into psychoanalysis led him into some fascinating interpretations of personality expressions which he called 'extraversion' and 'introversion' energy. It's surprising how closely these resemble the astrological understanding of positive and negative energy. See what you think when you read your own psychological profile later on.

If you can, imagine the twelve signs of the Zodiac as a symbolic representation of the various expressions of energy - as if the 'life force', symbolised by the planets, is diffused and refracted to express every kind of conceivable behavioural characteristic ever associated with man. The time of birth seems to dicate an individual's characteristics; so Astrology seems to have helped give birth to what we now know as psychological profiling.

Business and profiles.

Today, it's quite likely, if you apply for a position with any reasonable-sized company, that they will ask you not only to submit your current CV but also to fill out a psychological profile analysis sheet. This is to help them assess your suitability and your potential, the reason being that these 'profiles' are said to be well over 90% accurate. This is why companies are prepared to pay small fortunes to consultants to help them to recruit only the very best. And how do they find the best? They ask questions.

They will ask questions without you knowing the reason behind the question. For example:
Which word in each pair appeals to you more?
Gentle or Firm   Soft or Hard   Speak or Write   Sign or Symbol
Or: At parties, do you (A) sometimes get bored, or (B) always have fun?
Or: Would you rather work under someone who is (A) always kind, or
(B) always fair?

There are no 'right' or 'wrong' answers to the above questions. Your answers will help show how you look at things, and how you like to make decisions. If, from this, they decide you're not suitable, you won't even be given the chance of an interview. This is 'mind-blowing' stuff: do they really know that much about us? The answer, surprisingly, is: Yes, they do. Remember - they are said to be well over 90% accurate. However, turn this around, and if you are offered an interview after you have taken a psychological profile, then I would ask for more money, because you've already passed their test.

Michael Gauquelin (1928-1991).

Although a psychologist, he was also an exponent of modern statistical method. He was the first scientist to demonstrate a firm connection between the state of the Solar system, the time of birth and success in certain professions, and between specific planets and character traits. Yes, finally science does seem to be catching up. Gauquelin's findings centre exclusively upon the planets. He worked mostly in his native country France, mainly because every French citizen since the Revolution (1792) has had the exact time of birth recorded on their birth certificate, as well as the date and place.

Scientific experiment.

His first experiment was back in 1951, when he studied the birth details of well over five hundred members of the French Academy of Medicine. You would of course expect their times of birth to be random. However, that's not what he seems to have found. Way beyond any statistical coincidence, he discovered a strong connection with Mars and Saturn. At first, being quite sceptical, Gauquelin checked his results against a control group of people taken randomly from the register of births, and spread throughout the day. Their birth times made no planetary pattern whatsoever

By way of a double check, he looked at another five hundred plus doctors and came up with the same distinct Mars and Saturn connection, just as he had with the members of the Academy of Medicine. For most of his life, Gauquelin rejected traditional astrology, insisting instead that his research pointed to an entirely new pathway in science. Sadly, both then and now he's been thought of as an outcast, a heretic in the eyes of the scientific establishment.

Some amazing findings.

If he did appear to be onto something with his findings about eminent doctors, his subsequent discoveries suggest that this 'something' is pretty big. He researched notable writers, playwrights and journalists and found that they tended to have a connection with the Moon. Looking at actors, top executives and politicians he discovered that many more than average were born with a strong connection with Jupiter. His strongest findings of all, double the significant incidence of any other results, was the regularity with which Mars appeared in the natal charts of top-class athletes. If the pace of change continues then astrology will gain a more respectable, credible image as the twenty-first century progresses.

A sales manager's findings.

A sales manager quickly realised that over 75% of all his sales were being brought in by just three of the star signs: Aries, Gemini and Aquarius; and so he only hired people born under these star signs. It may not be as daft as it sounds, because all three signs are fast-moving and fast-thinking. Aries can be pushy and very competitive. Gemini and Aquarians are word spinners.

The Law of Polarity.

On the following pages I have outlined each sign of the Zodiac and conveniently placed on the same page its opposite star sign. If you imagine your own star sign as representing you - the 'you' others can see - then your opposite is representative of your inner world, a world others can't see. A world from within; your inner thoughts; a world only you can visit. Also, you will find your birthstones. If you find you are being drawn more to your opposite birthstone, you now have within this book an explanation of why. The combination of the two can, I believe, create a very powerful lucky talisman. It's the secret code, the Law of Polarity.

Negative traits

And finally, a word about the negative traits. So often I've heard people say that they don't like them or that these traits are nothing like them. Let me say, it's rare that you will see the negative traits in anybody unless life is really being cruel, or they are ill. Look upon them as God's gifts to survive; there are circumstances in everybody's life when these traits can become very valuable. Think about this: sometimes we need to be *manipulative, impatient, obsessive, restless, uncompromising, detached, dictatorial, materialistic* or *rebellious*. You may agree with me that without all these 'negative' traits Bob Geldoff would never have been able to create Band Aid, one of the most successful charity events of modern times.

See your local stockist for any Gemstones and Crystals mentioned in this publication. However, if you are having difficulty in obtaining any of the stones mentioned, we do offer our own mail order service and would be more than pleased to supply any of the stones listed.

For further details - write to: ROSEWOOD,
P.O. Box 219, Huddersfield, West Yorkshire. HD2 2YT
E-mail enquiries to: info@rosewood-gifts.co.uk
www.rosewood-gifts.co.uk

Aries - opposite star sign - **Libra**

Aries 21st March - 20th April   **Birthstone - Red Jasper**
The Ram   The First House (ruled by Mars)
Key Phrase - 'I have to know who I am'

Ariens have a straightforward and positive attitude to life. They need adventure and like to take risks. They are passionate and sexy people but can be aggressive and dominating. They are optimistic; they believe in and create their own luck, tackling life in an uncomplicated fashion. They are viewed as enterprising self-starters, naturally more impulsive, buoyant, communicative and sociable. Associated with the high-octane energy and enthusiasm of youth.

Positive traits - courageous, enthusiastic, independent, forthright. Negative traits - extravagant, impulsive, brash, selfish, impatient.
Element Fire
'Let's get on with it, now I am here'

*[Now read your opposite sign **Libra** for a fuller picture]*

Libra - opposite star sign - **Aries**

Libra 23rd Sept - 23rd Oct   **Birthstone - Green Aventurine**
The Scales   The Seventh House (ruled by Venus)
Key Phrase - 'I must justify my existence'

This is the sign of fair play and harmony. Librans are charmers who enjoy socialising and do not like to feel left out. They manage to appear calm in situations but can be indecisive. They are concerned with the realms of ideas. Libra symbolises the winds of change that bring fresh opportunities for growth, creative thought, exchanging and spreading information. They like the challenge of finding the balance between the needs of others and personal desire.

Positive traits - gracious, cheerful, charming, refined and diplomatic. Negative traits - manipulative, procrastinating and indecisive.
Element Air
'What is going on and why, I have to know?'

*[Now read your opposite sign **Aries** for a fuller picture]*

Taurus - opposite star sign - Scorpio

Taurus 21st April - 21st May   **Birthstone - Rose Quartz**
The Bull   The Second House (ruled by Venus)
Key Phrase - 'I need to see what I am'

Taureans are very loyal, sensible and reliable but need security and routine in their lives. They are passionate lovers but can be very possessive and sometimes stubborn. They are down-to-earth yet can be forceful. Their reliability in being constantly productive and precise leads them to top positions. Their creative and imaginative nature provides the ability to succeed in their chosen career. They can focus on using available resources to achieve practical ends.

Positive traits - sincere, reliable, faithful, solid and dependable.
Negative traits - obsessive, possessive, naive, obstinate and plodding.
Element Earth
'I don't yet know what it's all about, so I'll wait'

*[Now read your opposite sign **Scorpio** for a fuller picture]*

Scorpio - opposite star sign - Taurus

Scorpio 24th Oct - 22nd Nov   **Birthstone - Rhodonite**
The Scorpion   The Eighth House (ruled by Mars & Pluto)
Key Phrase - 'I am not alone'

Scorpios are energetic, intense, sensual people and concern themselves with deep hidden meanings, constantly seeking what lies beneath the surface. They have the ability to 'read between the lines'. They enjoy positions of power and tend to be strong-willed. They are secretive and jealous, can be possessive with partners, and enjoy active sexual relationships. They are protective, nurturing and compassionate.

Positive traits - resourceful, decisive, penetrating and focused.
Negative traits - resentful, vindictive, sarcastic, jealous and cunning.
Element Water
'To see if my first impressions are correct, I shall wait'

*[Now read your opposite sign **Taurus** for a fuller picture]*

Gemini - opposite star sign - **Sagittarius**

Gemini 22nd May - 21st June   **Birthstone - Black Onyx**
The Twins   The Third House (ruled by Mercury)
Key Phrase - 'I need to know why I am'

Very chatty, lively people who have a quick, light-hearted wit. They make good salespeople with their natural ability to sell and get on with people. Geminis can be charming, versatile and very often have the capacity to be bi-lingual. These excellent communicators have the ability to relate fascinating stories when speaking in public, although they can be impatient with others. At their best, their active, analytical mind can make sense of the relationship between things.

Positive traits - humorous, communicative, versatile and spontaneous.
Negative traits - restless, fickle, detached and inclined to exaggerate.
Element Air
'What is going on and why, I have to know'

*[Now read your opposite sign **Sagittarius** for a fuller picture]*

Sagittarius - opposite star sign - **Gemini**

Sagittarius 23rd Nov - 21st Dec   **Birthstone - Sodalite**
The Centaur   The Ninth House (ruled by Jupiter)
Key Phrase - 'I love to live'

These are the hunters who need freedom and stimulation. Sagittarians are enthusiastic and fun-loving, and have a thirst for knowledge. They are optimists, always open to new experiences, and love adventure and travel. They need a lot of understanding, as they can be unreliable and restless, especially within the confines of a relationship. They do, however, usually achieve emotional happiness and material success. Their luck sees them through.

Positive traits - frank, logical, kind, generous, optimistic and honest.
Negative traits - extravagant, quarrelsome, blunt and dictatorial.
Element Fire
'Let's get on with it, now I am here'

*[Now read your opposite sign **Gemini** for a fuller picture]*

Cancer - opposite star sign - Capricorn

Cancer 22nd June - 22nd July   **Birthstone - Mother of Pearl**
The Crab   The Fourth House (ruled by the Moon)
Key Phrase - 'I must know my origins'

Cancerians are very nice, charming, caring and sensitive people. However, they do have a tendency to worry, although more often they are self-assured and resourceful. They also tend to be extremely sensitive to the moods and emotional undercurrents around them. They are very faithful, making very good long-term friends. They are receptive to the needs of partners and those close to them. They can comprehend that which is not necessarily seen; they have great insight.

Positive traits - industrious, thrifty, loyal, sympathetic and sensitive. Negative traits - secretive, capricious, cloying, touchy and clingy.
Element Water
'To see if my first impressions are correct, I shall wait'

*[Now read your opposite sign **Capricorn** for a fuller picture]*

Capricorn - opposite star sign - Cancer

Capricorn 22nd Dec- 20th Jan   **Birthstone - Obsidian Snowflake**
The Goat   The Tenth House (ruled by Saturn)
Key Phrase - 'Nil Desperandum' ('Never give up')

Capricorns are ambitious, hard working, independent individuals, empire-builders who enjoy good taste and achieve success later in life. They have a tendency to be bossy when pursuing prestige and power. They can be stubborn in their need for financial security and stability. However, they have good organising skills and are cautious and realistic, with high standards. They are scrupulous, fearless and sure-footed, traits that lead to becoming self-made, successful people.

Positive traits - profound, efficient, ambitious and hard working. Negative traits - gloomy, materialistic, arrogant and intolerant.
Element Earth
'I don't yet know what it's all about, so I'll wait'

*[Now read your opposite sign **Cancer** for a fuller picture]*

Leo - opposite star sign - **Aquarius**

Leo 23rd July - 23rd Aug   **Birthstone - Tiger Eye**
The Lion   The Fifth House (ruled by the Sun)
Key Phrase - 'I am capable of becoming more'

Leos are born leaders and organisers who are creative and charismatic. They always enjoy life to the full. They are generous and like spending money. They are warm and enthusiastic. Although they can be dominating and vain, Leos tend to make it to the top. They are creative, honest and loyal, courageous to the point of self-sacrifice, with a pride in their work and their home. They show great strength when under a lot of pressure or when in a crisis. Leos have a sunny disposition.

Positive traits - hospitable, affectionate, regal and magnanimous. Negative traits - self-centred, uncompromising, vain and domineering.
Element Fire
'Let's get on with it, now I am here'

*[Now read your opposite sign **Aquarius** for a fuller picture]*

Aquarius - opposite star sign - **Leo**

Aquarius 21st Jan - 19th Feb   **Birthstone - Blue Agate**
The Water Carrier   The Eleventh House (ruled by Saturn & Uranus)
Key Phrase - 'I belong to the family of man'

Aquarians make excellent friends; they are understanding and faithful. They are complex characters, original, magnetic, inventive and visionary. They are witty, chatty and sharp with independent minds. They can appear eccentric at times. They are communicative, thoughtful, caring and scientific, hence their complex characters. Aquarian ideas may be unusual and original, but once formed they tend to remain fixed and focused, which shows their independence of thought and action.

Positive traits - trustworthy, caring, friendly and broad-minded. Negative traits - unpredictable, moody, rebellious and impersonal.
Element Air
'What is going on and why, I have to know'

*[Now read your opposite sign **Leo** for a fuller picture]*

Virgo - opposite star sign - Pisces

Virgo 24th Aug - 22nd Sept   **Birthstone - Carnelian**
The Virgin   The Sixth House (ruled by Mercury)
Key Phrase - 'I must always strive for perfection'

Virgos are workers, practical and neat in every way. They can be perfectionists and are capable of giving self-sacrificing service to others, although they may be critical of them. They are very genuine, powerful people but they tend to worry, although they are the ones who can improve stability and create order from apparent chaos. Virgos almost crave the opportunity to serve others and take charge. They have a gentleness with the helpless, and are sympathetic and well-organised.

Positive traits - painstaking, analytical, studious and considerate.
Negative traits - detached, sceptical, prone to worry, and cynical.
Element Earth
'I don't yet know what it's all about, so I'll wait'

*[Now read your opposite sign **Pisces** for a fuller picture]*

Pisces 20th Feb - 20th March   **Birthstone - Amethyst**
The Fish   The Twelfth House (ruled by Jupiter & Neptune)
Key Phrase - 'I wish I could come back some other time'

Pisceans are the dreamers, creative and imaginative, but lacking confidence. They are very loving, caring, sensitive and kind; they are lovers of peace. They may lack ambition, can be vague and indecisive, and sometimes lack the insight for promotion through their inability to promote themselves. They like discipline and are ideal for tasks where regular duties are called for. They are trusting, hospitable and will help anyone in distress. Pisces is a sign of a 'healer'.

Positive traits - unassuming, courteous, imaginative, gentle and lenient.
Negative traits - apologetic, changeable and self-pitying.
Element Water
'To see if my first impressions are correct, I shall wait'

*[Now read your opposite sign **Virgo** for a fuller picture]*

NOTES

Welcome to the world of Rosewood

An extract from a 'thank- you' letter for one of my books.

"I realised just how much you really had indeed understood me and my need for direction and truly have allowed me the confidence and strength to know and believe I can achieve whatever I want in life"

If you like natural products, hand-crafted gifts including Gemstone jewellery, objects of natural beauty – the finest examples from Mother Nature, tinged with an air of Mystery – then we will not disappoint you.
For those who can enjoy that feeling of connection with the esoteric nature of Gemstones and Crystals, then our 'Power for Life – Power Bracelets could be ideal for you.
Each bracelet comes with its own guide explaining a way of thinking that's so powerful it will change your life and the information comes straight from the Bible.
e.g. read Mark 11: 22

We regularly give inspirational talks on
Crystal Power – fact or fiction?
A captivating story about the world's fascination with natural gemstones and crystals and how the Placebo effect explains the healing power of gemstones and crystals – it's intriguing.
And it's available on a CD

To see our full range of books, jewellery and gifts
including CD's and DVD'S
Visit our web site - www.rosewood-gifts.co.uk
To see our latest videos go to 'You Tube'
and type in Rosewood Gifts.